Mervin Chief Calf

ASSIMINATION BRIDGE

Assimination Bridge

Wholesale discounts for book orders are available through Ingram Distributors.

Tellwell Talent
www.tellwell.ca

ISBN
Paperback: 978-1-77302-958-0

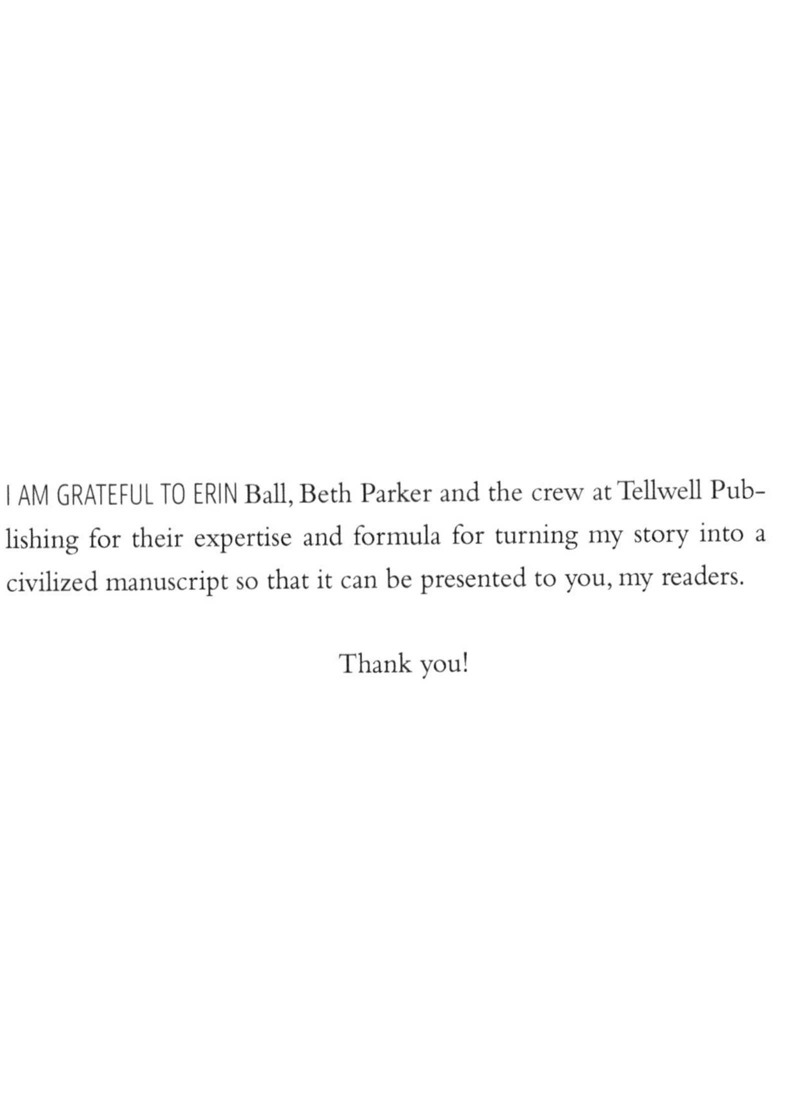

I AM GRATEFUL TO ERIN Ball, Beth Parker and the crew at Tellwell Publishing for their expertise and formula for turning my story into a civilized manuscript so that it can be presented to you, my readers.

Thank you!

ASSIMINATION BRIDGE

1

ON THIS BRIDGE I SPENT most of my childhood and youth. It was a span connecting the native reserve and white county land. It was in a river valley that snaked westward and northeast. In June the sun rose over the northeast side parallel to the river.

Westward on the county side of the gravel road the area was heavily forested from the river's edge up to the cliffs and precipices standing guard. Northeastward alongside the river on the county side there was a small tract of farmland. Where the river turned eastward there was a series of hills overlooking the meandering water.

The rows of stubble and bales left behind on the small farmland, was in stark contrast to the prairie pasture land on the native reserve. County land was linear with straw bales neatly deposited and spaced apart evenly. On the reserve side wild roses, sage, sweet grass, and chokecherry bushes ruled the holistic side of the reserve.

In the beginning when I was starting grade 1 the bridge was an escape from the boredom and stagnation of reserve life. From that point on I would cross this bridge back and forth until my last year in high school.

The bridge a single lane wooden plank structure held in place by concrete pillars was neutral to the two worlds it connected. As a kid I would stare at the current below it made me feel like I was going somewhere. The river flow forded around the concrete pillars giving the illusion the bridge was actually moving. It was hypnotizing and I would catch myself staring down at the illusion for what felt like an eternity.

After my first few visits to the bridge when I was still in grade 1 I met Em. I was on the bridge and she emerged from the trees on the county side of the bridge. We would go down to the river's edge and find rocks that looked like toy cars or shaped like toy guns. On the bridge Em and I played with our toys for hours bringing them to life with our imagination.

When we got tired of our toys we would go back down to the river and find more rocks that were molded and shaped by our imagination. Most of the time we would leave our rocks on the steel rail of the bridge at the end of the day. She would leaveon the county side and I would leave on the reserve side until the next day.

That's how it would be those first few years on the bridge. Em and I would meet and play oblivious to the traffic that crossed the bridge every now and then.

From grade 1 and on, a bus picked us up and we commuted across the bridge into town to the white catholic school. Because we lived on the outer edge of the reserve we were bussed in to the local white school system. The reserve school was on the other side where the majority of residents lived.

Only a handful of households dotted the east end river valley of the reserve. Ours was the only house with children the others were elderly residents. Their children had come and gone. These folks lived their lives in this valley never venturing beyond the surrounding hills except for groceries and water. Back and forth for twelve years I crossed this bridge. Every day I was exposed to two worlds and the bridge became my haven from both sides.

Em and I would escape and imagine we were worlds away. All we had was the bridge and our vivid imagination. When we were superheroes she used to say she had real super powers and she was going to save our people. I went along with it because we were just playing and having fun.

Em and I remained friends up until the day I left to pursue a higher education. I would tell her about my dreams of leaving the reserve to make something of my life.

With my increasing exposure to the white school each passing year Em and I started to grow apart slowly by ideology. She was every bit a native girl with her long dark hair in a pony tail. She never used make up because she was natural and native in every way. Em always wore her jean jacket and faded jeans. When she got older in her teens she started smoking. Usually kids started smoking through peer pressure but I never saw Em with anyone but me. I never smoked or pressured her to start smoking.

It was when Em started participating in native ceremonies did she start smoking. Her Uncle was heavily involved in the native rituals and ceremonies he was one of the last powerful people of the reserve. He raised her and became his apprentice in ritual and ceremonial power. Em never talked about it because if I wanted to know about it I had to participate with her in the ceremonies.

Em would hunt for sustenance and sometimes she would bring her uncle's rifle with her to the bridge when we would hang out. Those last few years she began to converse with me in the native tongue more frequently. She would start inviting me to go hunting with her. I refused her because I believed her world was disappearing. She was just as opposed to my past times of watching hockey on TV and listening to classic rock on my 8 track.

One of the things we did agree on was the stagnation that afflicted the reserve. Another one of our shared vexations was the way the reserve was being run by the leaders. She wanted things to change and so did I. Em wanted the people to change and I believed the system was to blame.

I said I could change things by being an example. If I could make it off the reserve and prosper then others would give it a try. Her argument was the people needed to hang on to the culture.

I argued there was no pure culture left. I told her simply knowing the language and knowing the ceremonies was not enough to call it a culture. I said it was all or nothing when it came to culture. We couldn't be full blooded natives when we wore blue jeans and drove pick-up trucks to bingo in the city.

I told Em there was something wrong when you look in the obits and see natives in their teens, 20's, and 30's, while the white people in the obits are in their 80's and 90's.

With only a small group of councillor's running the reserve there was no accountability. The white governments had oppositions to keep the leaders in check for transparency. I told Em there were many things wrong with the system and that needed to change.

She replied, "there is a way for the reserve to become whole again. It has to start with this bridge."

I disagreed with her vehemently I said the bridge was the reason I was going to make it out of the reserve.

Em said, "the bridge stands for more than that".

I told her to explain that and she refused to go into it any further. She said I would understand if I joined her in learning about the teachings she learned from her uncle.

I said I was leaving and wasn't coming back. Em never argued it was I that pushed her but she never pushed back all, she did was smile. It was a smile that suggested she knew more than she led on. This was the feeling I got but she never divulged anything.

It concerned her that things on the reserve were going to pieces but not to the point that it overwhelmed her. Em never got overwhelmed in front of me she had her life and that was all that mattered to her. What was left of our way of life was all that mattered to Em.

"You're waiting for a savior to come along?"

"I'm waiting for something and I believe it will come," she replied.

"You make things happen that's what I believe".

"I believe in that too," she replied.

"You won't tell me who your savior is you might be waiting a long time Em".

"You want to know who my savior is come back with me to my uncle and I'll show you".

"I already told you Em I'm not getting involved in your mystical ways".

"That's the only way you're going to know things about our people that's all that's left. Like you said you have to go out there and make things happen".

"You're twisting my words Em my belief is out there on the bridge. The knowledge I seek is out there at the university".

This is how it went that last summer before I left the reserve for the university in the city. Em and I pointed and counterpointed we volleyed back and forth our ideologies. All it did was make me more determined to leave and prove to her that my goal was the way out.

That was years ago decades ago.

My how things have changed.

That was the last time I saw Em and set foot on the reserve.

So much had happened and yet nothing had happened.

2

SITTING ON THE FLOOR IN my small basement apartment it's late into Sunday night. I can't sleep for longer than a couple of hours anymore. When I do finally nod off the empty desperate spirits come and they want what's left, of my energy. Emptiness wants company and what I have left they want to ravenously engulf like rabid vampires.

My years at the university is such a distant memory. Sitting amongst fellow professional students I was somewhat of a novel anomaly. The rich white kids embraced me like I was one of their own. They liked to drink and smoke drugs so I started indulging because I now identified with these upper class hard partying students.

There was one small problem they kept their grades up above the average. I was so obsessed with the status of being in university I never took care of my grades.

Volumes of required reading for each class piled up under empty beer cans and empty vodka bottles. I tried the overnight cramming that seemed to work for the other students. It didn't work for me because I wasn't that type of learner. Repetition for me was the key I had to do things over and again for it to sink in. I would have to read chapters over and again for it to make sense to me. With each passing day the volumes grew making it impossible to understand the information and retain it.

It didn't matter because I was accepted and celebrated at the university pub. This is where I belonged with like minded colleagues who treated me like their equal.

The celebrity status lasted three semesters then I was unceremoniously kicked out of school for failed grades. The rest of the elite kept going pursuing their degrees. None of them called to see how I was doing. I didn't grace their hallowed halls of higher learning anymore and now I wasn't good enough anymore.

I wasn't going home like this after being on this high of higher learning.

The plan now was to work so I can keep my basement apartment. When I could reapply I would start over and concentrate on my studies.

After a series of jobs the plan to go back to school kept getting postponed and delayed. Months passed and when it was time to reapply I couldn't get away from the paycheck, pub scene, and the new friends I made from work.

Years started passing by and my wage and penchant for getting high started to increase. I was now being accepted by the white working class and in our weekends in the pub.

I was convinced that this is where I belonged not with the rich kids at the university. I was the anomaly again this time with the white working class. They had never worked with a native who actually stuck with the job for more than two weeks.

I got in at the very bottom level at this production plant facility because another guy failed to show up. I was not expected to last but as time went by I started exceeding the supervisor's expectations.

This was no different than the white school it was a matter of adapting to the routine. In the beginning it was physical labor putting product onto pallets of a production line. After several months the probationary period came and went and I was offered a position.

I began to move up the ladder going from laborer to forklift operator. From there I moved up to machine operator and the paycheck began to be significant.

This time I had found my niche. It wasn't exactly as I planned, it turned out to be a back-up plan I didn't anticipate.

Why hadn't this world of computers, moving parts, compressed air, and mass production not worked on the reserve? I couldn't see the problem because I had spent half my life in the white world.

I had been immersed in this world since I was six years old. With nothing back home in terms of opportunities, employment, and security the choice wasn't hard about where I wanted to be.

The years went by and I just quietly went along, the reserve just a distant fading memory with each passing day. Just like the university where I wasn't focused on the long term plan, in my job I wasn't focused on the long term plan. My coworkers paid mortgages, saved for retirement, paid into bonds, and grew nest eggs.

I spent time in the bars and casinos just like my coworkers the only difference is they put money away and I lived paycheck to paycheck.

In every sense I was stagnating like the people on the reserve. From that perspective I was standing still and not preparing for the future. Life insurance was another policy I didn't understand, what is money good for if you weren't around to use it.

I had no dependents, no spouse, and this business of a will was too grim. This business of dying was a tragedy on the reserve and in the white world it was a business.

It was that part of me from the reserve of not looking at the future that prevented me from planning. There was no such thing as time on the reserve and nobody planned on the reserve because there was nothing to plan. That part of me was still engrained in me. Planning was something white people did. They never talked about it; they didn't acted on it in my presence. It was a private affair.

Months and years went by and I had nothing to show for my efforts. I didn't make it off the reserve I stagnated just like they did back home.

By this time I had maxed out credit cards, payday loan debts, I was behind in rent, I was drinking heavy, getting hooked on pain medication, and I was missing work.

I couldn't sleep anymore everything was starting to close in on me. Bills were overdue and the pay day loan people were calling me all the time.

The phone started ringing more and more. It was someone that wanted something and I had run out of things to give. I had taken beyond my means and couldn't give back. The things that motivated me to leave the reserve had caught up to me. Stagnation and desolation found me after all these years because I led them to me through years of excess.

Don't know if I'll sleep tonight those spirits are waiting for me. They are drawn to those who are at the end because they recognize their own.

I left the reserve on my own terms and now I have no terms no resolve and there is no place to go. I'll leave the TV on with the sound turned down low.

Tonight the spirits are going to have to wait. I'm going to stay up and try to figure out what to do. I want to know why my initial plan didn't work out. I'm going to light a candle and turn off the lights.

There is a reason why things turned out this way. I'll make some more coffee and unhook the phone.

Who am I?

3

I HAD PLENTY OF LEFTOVER note paper from my days at the university. I decided to put it to use and began scribbling ideas. Establish what is certain.

Reserve people had nowhere to go except within the boundaries of the reserve. They were raised in extended family households. They went to school on the reserve and if they were fortunate enough gained employment on the reserve. They had their own fire dept, own police dept, and leaders to run their own administration to keep them functioning.

So why were there rampant drug and alcohol abuse, and early death, why were kids being left at home neglected. One issue spiraled and merged with another spiraling crisis. A perfect storm was brewing and the waves had become so great until the problem was too big to face.

Looking back I survived because I would retreat to the bridge separating the two worlds. Another factor was our relative isolation from the other communities.

On the bridge the occasional vehicle would pass by. They never gave me a second look I was like a permanent fixture on the bridge.

When bingo became all the rage a line of cars and trucks crossed the bridge into the city at certain times of the day and evening. The dust from the gravel road wouldn't settle for an hour after the last vehicle crossed the bridge.

The sun rays were starting to peer in from my basement window when I began to make some sort of semblance of my situation. My times on the bridge with Em kept coming back flooding me with memories.

We had so many discussions on the bridge I wondered how she was doing. She must've found a man by now and was raising a family.

When you have no place to go you spiral into nothingness and that was the gist of it all. All those years away spiraled into where I am now. I let desolation and stagnation become the norm unknowingly because deep down that's who I was. I could not shed the skin of my true identity.

Em and I spent all that time on the bridge that we made it our identity. I was the bridge because I belonged to neither side.

On one side there is the fading way of life like the language, customs, values, and the ceremonies. On the other side there is the influence and assimilation of ideas coming from the white world.

The white side brought Saturday night hockey on TV. The white world brought fast food and the convenience of a service society. Native culture and white society are pulling the natives in opposite directions.

I kept scribbling down these ideas not realizing the sun was making its way up from beyond the neighborhood.

I had another coffee.

It was all about the bridge.

Reserve life was the bridge with nothing underneath in the way of an identity. The only thing that moved on the reserve was the current below the bridge just like the passage of time.

Assimination Brige

The bridge was a state of mind of sorts on the reserve. With one way leading to a past that can't be breached, and on the other side an invading world natives retreated to the bridge. Just like Em and I when we were kids, natives also looked down at the water from their space on the bridge. They watched the water wade past them and believed the pillars fording the river were a sign of resistance. They had resolved to wait out their lives looking down at the illusion from the bridge because that was all there was left to do. This is where the two sides of the bridge could not touch them.

On the bridge you are the conscientious objector of the world around you, so you don't have to take part in it.

Once you belong to the bridge you are a member for the duration, all you can do is hold on. The blessing in disguise is that most members do not realize they are a part of this absurd middle world. The bridge rules were laid down when the whites landed on our shores. They unleashed the secret germ warfare called small pox and shook our hands in friendship.

No one knew as mother held onto her little baby that the little one was already taken from her arms. She smiled and nursed a smiling disembodied spirit that felt like a real child.

Buffalo you were a great provider but you are not part of the plan of the bridge rules. We won't be needing your hide because there will be little uniforms replacing your warmth.

There will be fast food outlets to take your place Buffalo. You can now take your place in the written archives stored away in some distant metropolis owing allegiance to tourists.

The bridge is the only place where we are not part of the ground, the sky or water. It is truly a stagnant point of reference where we have been waiting since first contact to find out the fate of our people.

The bridge was created the moment the whites landed on our shores. The native way of life ended the true culture the true identity began to disappear starting with the disease we had no immunity for.

The bridge mentality began settling in with each new generation. On one side our true people were now gone into the past. On the other side was the white world with all its linear strokes of time governed by its institutions.

The white side was planned out from birth to the last days in the old folks home. From planned birth, planned-parenthood, school, work, mortgages, rearing and letting go, vacations, weddings, retirement, and then the final days.

This was waiting on the white side of the bridge.

To some varying degree we were still a nation, along the way our culture got assimilated.

The forces on both sides have molded a new identity for us.

We are now the assimination and our new homeland is the bridge. We are an assimilated nation the assimination.

My identity now made sense.

Even though I left the assimination bridge two decades ago I couldn't get away from my identity. I deluded myself into thinking I was getting away from the stagnation and desolation. I brought it with me; here I sit with nothing to show for all those years of work and school.

I was sad and at the same time relieved that I found an answer to my identity. The phone started ringing once I plugged it back in. It was either my boss, landlord, or a creditor because I was so far behind.

I needed to leave this linear existence because it was slowly leading to my destruction.

The whites got a head start because they have lived this linear existence for years long before they landed on these shores. They have built an immunity against drugs and alcohol and manage to live their lives without falling apart. It's part of their DNA, it's built into their genes so they have a predisposition and manage to live their linear lives.

The holistic side of me from the assimination bridge is still in its infancy. We have to learn to take the holistic and linear and combine it in our assimination existence.

I have lived the linear life for years and now I have to relive the holistic side.

I need to find a way to bring the two sides together.

Em knew I was coming back she had the foresight to know that I wouldn't last. Maybe with the powers she had she could look into the future who knows?

The old homestead has been abandoned for years. I think I'm going to hitch a ride back home and relearn the holistic way. I'll get Em to teach me the ways she wanted me to learn.

4

I WENT COLD TURKEY WITH the whole linear existence of the white world. Codeine, alcohol, casino's, and the rat race were now at an abrupt end.

Using my last paycheck I went downtown and got the power hooked up at the house on the reserve. The heat and running water I can take care of later. I can draw water from the river and I think the outhouse is still standing.

I wasn't going to pack anything from my basement apartment. I wanted my landlord to think I was away on a trip and would be back.

Once he was onto my plan he wasn't going to hunt me down on the reserve. I wanted to leave everything I amassed in the linear world to stay in the linear world. I didn't have much a small cassette stereo, some books, and a TV. The big stuff the table, couch, and bed I was going to leave behind.

I dusted off my school book bag to carry some clothes and some non perishables for a few days.

In the old house I was going to create a thesis on how to combine and define the assimination bridge existence with Em.

It may have seemed like I was running out on my linear world that allowed me to survive all this time. It took the over comsumption of the excesses of this world to realize I wasn't going to survive it.

The assimination people needed time to get used to the pitfalls of the white linear world. The whites had a century of a head start to control their linear world.

I needed to create a philosophy, an instruction to use as a blue print for my assimination ideology.

First things first I needed to walk out of my apartment for the last time with only a backpack to show for it all. By the time I got out to the reserve later today the electricity should be hooked up.

It was now almost noon and the afternoon bingo players were filing into town from the reserve. Their route into town took them past the old house and across the bridge.

By 3:00 pm I would catch the city bus and transfer to the south end of the city. Once there the highway is a short walk that leads to the turn off to the gravel road leading to the reserve. Once on the highway I could catch a ride with one of the bingo players heading back home to the reserve.

I had a few hours to kill so I decided to try and sleep. I laid down on the couch and closed my eyes. With my eyes closed I wasn't asleep yet and I can already sense these hungry sentient beings lurking.

They had been visiting me now for quite some time. From the time I started realizing I was getting bled dry in the linear world, these energies started getting attracted to my semi-conscious state.

While I laid there on my bed I could sense them standing all around me watching over me. This is why I could only sleep for a couple of hours at a time. I wasn't sure if these entities wanted to take me away or if they were guardians.

I could only surmise that they were energies that didn't survive the state I was in when they were alive. I think these were spirits from the assimination bridge. I wonder if the whites ever got visited like this by spirits. Maybe they did in the past when drugs and alcohol were first introduced into their world. Centuries have passed and their immunity to these beings had allowed them to sleep without a conscience no matter what.

It's a good thing I could only sleep for a few hours in the middle of the day. These spirits were powerless when the sun was up. In the night when they came I was scared because the night was where they belonged.

In the night these energies were in their world and I didn't want them to get to me. These past few weeks I only slept for a couple of hours during the day when these entities were powerless against me.

I hadn't been at work for a few days and my coworkers and boss were probably wondering what became of me.

It didn't seem like sleep because I was aware of the presence around me. A few hours did go by and my preoccupation made it seem like only a short time. If the clock said a few hours went by then they did.

It was time to go.

According to plan I got on the street bus and transferred to the furthest end of the city. I got off the bus and from there it was a few miles on the highway before the reserve gravel road turn off. I started walking and was clear of the city limit when the bus I rode for twelve years zoomed past me.

There were lots of small kids on the bus. No older kids were in the bus just like I figured. The older kids usually dropped out by junior high.

I had a few miles still to cover so I kept going. I was almost at the gravel turn off when a pickup truck pulled up beside me. It was always the ones that got lucky at bingo that were feeling magnanimous.

The ones that lost money didn't stop for anyone on the road.

"Where you headed?" the man said.

"To the reserve just down in the valley," I replied.

"Get in," the driver said.

I got in and we turned off toward the reserve. We didn't say anything for awhile. The driver kept glancing over trying to see if he recognized me.

I knew it was coming so I decided to keep quiet. Eventually he asked.

"Now I know who you are. You're the kid who used to hang out at the bridge years ago. Am I right?"

I nodded.

"That was some years ago what are you doing now?"

"I was working in the city but now I'm moving back home."

"No one's lived at your home for years. It'll be good to see that farm light turned on again after all this time."

We were heading down the hill to the valley and not soon enough. I wanted to ask about Em but at the same time I didn't want to engage in any conversation.

"I'll get off at the bridge," I said.

"Yeah sure," the driver slowed to a halt on the bridge.

I got off and I had to ask.

"Does Em still live around here?"

"Who?"

"Em, the girl that was on the bridge with me."

"I never saw anyone on the bridge with you," the driver replied.

"What!" I didn't understand his reply.

"I saw you on the bridge ever since you were a little boy. I never saw anyone with you."

I slowly nodded and moved away from the truck to the rail. The driver had a puzzled look on his face as he drove away. My face probably looked just as puzzling because what he said didn't make sense.

Em and I spent years together on this bridge. A cloud of dust followed the half ton as it made its way up the reserve side of the valley.

Maybe it wasn't a good idea to stay on the bridge. I made my way to the house before anyone else knew I was home.

5

THE HOME I GREW UP in has been empty for years. Everyone from the past that I knew have grown up and moved on. My parents separated and moved back with their families. The home was empty and it was only a matter of time before the pigeons and swallows took over the home.

The grass had since swallowed up the road leading to the home. I cut a path through the prairie wool to a home I thought I'd never see again.

I remembered waiting at the road for the bus when I knew full well I had missed it. I missed it because the drinking ran all night and I didn't get much sleep. I waited at the road crouched up against some brush that provided a wind break. This also hid me from vision from the house so it appeared that I got on the bus. I got comfortable and fell asleep. When I awoke the sun was free from the hill horizon and it was warm. The partying had died down so I went back home.

I put my lunch in the fridge amidst the snoring sprawled out drunks. I took one last look at the empty bottles and ash trays before I headed for the bridge. I could see Em on the bridge just like she always was when I headed that way.

I arrived at the house the grass had grown wild all around hiding the fast food wrappers and broken bottles. I noticed a crack had developed in the foundation leading to where there once was a basement window. The basement window was replaced with a board an attempt to seal a broken window. The gap from the crack was wide enough for a small critter to get in.

Because stagnation and desolation never changed anything the key I held onto all these years still opened the locked door. I flipped the light switch and the bulb responded. The power company was prompt in getting the power hooked up.

For now I was just going to set up the kitchen as my living space. The stove would be my heat source for now. I packed enough non perishables and bottled water for few days. I needed a few days to figure out what I was going to do next. I was AWOL, MIA, and even TBA to the world I was once a part of.

I had nothing now but an idea. The assimination bridge theory was all I had as a faint hope. The withdrawal from my previous life and its excesses began to creep up my spine.

A cold sweat began to form along my brow. My body and mind wanted to be fed the poisons I had endured for years. While I had the energy I formed a bed with some cushions on the kitchen floor. The kitchen oven provided enough heat for my space.

There was a window facing the bridge that you could see out from the kitchen. Every once in awhile I took a peek out, there was no sign of Em.

There was a door that led to the porch area and basement stairs to the side. I plugged up the bottom of the door with some old clothes to prevent any heat from escaping. A few hours had gone by and the evening rush of bingo players began to make their way back to town.

The procession left the gravel dirt on the road clinging to the air.

The long shadows cast by the rolling hills all around began to seep into the river valley. Soon the farm light would turn on after years of darkness. It was now starting to get dark in the kitchen but the light coming from the oven element was enough for now.

I didn't want to draw any attention but the farm light was starting to wake up and it was giving me away. Maybe with the road still buried in deep grass no one would try to turn in and investigate.

I made some tea in the hopes that it would help with the withdrawal symptoms. Sweat and body aches started to engulf me. I went into a fetal position that seemed to ease the pain in my back as the withdrawal concentrated on weak spots in my body. It wasn't going to let me go just like that. My body and mind wanted the alcohol and codeine it had depended on for years.The addiction wanted to be fed all I could do was hold on while it clawed away.

In town there was a liquor store and drug store only blocks away. Out here in the desolation of the assimination bridge there was no escape, no relief, and no reprieve.

I got up with the shakes now working their way through my body and took a sip from the tea. I lay back down and started taking deep slow breaths and tried to calm myself from the involuntary shakes coming on.

I closed my eyes and continued to breathe slow and deep.All those sleepless nights must've caught up to me I don't remember dozing off.

Those deprived spirits came back. They seemed to have gained more power from my desperate state. I was in a weak state and they were standing all around me. I could only make out their silhouetted forms feeding off my vulnerable and exposed life force.

I couldn't move and they just stood over me looking at me. I could feel my heart racing I wanted so much to wake up but I couldn't. They didn't have to do anything they waited for my fear to overcome my frail energy so they can gorge on what was left.

With no resolve I thought 'that's it' I give up. If this is it then they can take my decrepit body and energy. If it's going to sate their appetite then they can have my soul for what it's worth.

When my fear changed to despair the lost souls began to back away from me. It was like something was driving them away repelling them from my energy.

I stirred from my sleep when I heard something from behind the porch door. The porch door led to the basement and the front door. I opened my eyes but didn't make a move or sound. I waited for the sound again.

Outside I could hear the vehicles passing by on their way home. That meant bingo was over and it was around 10 pm. I just laid there my neck drenched in sweat. The dim light from the oven was just enough to expose the immediate area of the kitchen. I decided to light a candle for a little more light. I turned off the oven it was getting too hot. The tea was cold but I gulped it down anyway.

The window facing the bridge allowed the headlights to peer into the kitchen as they descended into the river valley. The candle light was only a little brighter then the oven light maintaining my subterfuge from the bingo passer byes.

Something drove those desperate spirits away or maybe the noise that roused me was enough to break me free. I stared at the ceiling still not sure if I made the right move in coming out here.

The flickering candle induced crazy shadows from objects it couldn't move like the table and chairs. I thought about Em and wondered how she was doing.

The noise that stirred me from my sleep broke the silence again. It was coming from the porch. I remembered the crack in the cement foundation it was big enough for a critter to get in.

The sound turned into a scraping sound against the door. It was definitely a critter of some sort. Maybe it made the porch its home and was returning from hunting. It was getting in from the dangers of the night just like what I was doing.

I waited.

I wasn't going to open the door and find a pissed off Badger staring back at me. More time passed and the critter gave itself up.

The cat meowed and scratched at the door again.

I drew a sigh a relief it was only a cat. I opened the door just a little and a paw slipped through grabbing at the air. I opened the door and the cat slipped in to bask in the warm kitchen. In the candle light it looked like a young calico about a year old. I went back to my makeshift bed and the cat purred and brushed up against me.

"So you're the one the spirits were afraid of," I said.

I got up and found a saucer in the cupboard. I poured some water from my bottle and the cat lapped a drink. I also had some bologna and gave some to the cat. I lay back down and the gentle purring sound was enough so I fell back asleep. I was able to sleep through the rest of the night the first time in a long time.

I slept because the spirits never came back. The calico curled up at the edge of the bed by my feet. I still didn't have an appetite so I made some tea and took a better look at my guardian. The cat had brown, white, and black fur and a cross between a short hair and all out bushy feline.

I turned the oven back on sometime during the night the candle burnt out and it was getting cold again. It was a good sleep I didn't even notice the cold until I got up. I don't think I had a dream it was a pure sleep that my body and mind needed.

I sat at the table where I had my note book where I had my scribbled notes on my theory.

I had the right idea in the beginning by leaving to try my luck with the white side of the bridge. All those years spent in school and work in the city I thought made a difference. I thought I was leading a trail that others would be able to follow.

I took the assimination bridge with me and didn't even know it. The reason it could not work was because there was no way of bridging the holistic and linear side.

We were trapped on the assimination bridge with two opposite worlds on each side. In my note book I drew half a box and half a circle. I connected the two and there it was. Two shapes that could not be whole so I drew them again facing the other way. These two halves facing the other way best describe the identity of the natives on the reserve.

You either had to be linear, a complete box or a holistic a complete circle. I tried to connect the two and exist in the white world but it didn't work.

Even if the linear world eventually took over the reserve the holistic side of our culture would not completely disappear. Just like the incongruent halves they would only co-exist one side never taking over the other. If the holistic side ever took over the linear side was everywhere and established it was here to stay.

It would remain as the holistic side struggling to survive and the linear side forever encroaching. It has been that way since first contact eons ago. That was the equation this was the fact.

Even though I could speak and understand my native language there was no use for it in the linear world. There was no use for it in the holistic world either because every generation since the original generation needed to speak the linear language to communicate with the next generation, and so on.

I drew the opposing halves again.

In the middle I drew a line to symbolize the assimination bridge where I existed. This line was my new homeland away from the two opposing forces. Both sides wanted me for different reasons. The linear side wanted me to buy into their way of living. The holistic side wanted me to hold on to what was left of the native way of life.

I could not relent to either so I resisted and retreated to the assimination bridge. For my efforts the two worlds turned their backs on me. I wanted to be whole again but there was nowhere to turn. All there was to do was wait, and this was the very essence of the assimilation identity.

All everyone could do on the assimination bridge was wait.

Why we were waiting was still uncertain at this time.

Since first contact that is all we have been doing because that is all we can do when two worlds want all of you.

6

WAITING FOR WHAT IS THE question.

On the assimination bridge lives go on. Chief and council administer services to sustain the waiting. In the interim there is the bus driver bringing kids to school. There is the water truck delivering water to independent water wells to the homes. The grader operator fixes the gravel road when it needs it, yet he is waiting.

There are various attempts at independent business ventures. Some float for awhile and others fail and they return to the waiting.

These are attempts to take the holistic and linear offerings to formulate some sort of life. It ends up being a wait because the two sides don't offer enough for a foot hold.

Some get tired of waiting.

They dull the waiting with alcohol and drugs. This is a precursor to the eventual end of the waiting.

The calico started meowing from the living room window. I went to investigate and the cat was on the sill staring outside. I looked outside and at the bridge there was a figure leaning against the rail.

"Thanks for letting me know," I said and was going to pet the cat but it was gone. I looked around it was nowhere in sight.

I put on my jacket and shoes the cat was still nowhere to be found.

"Here kitty!" I called but still it didn't come around.

The cat would be okay so I turned off the oven and headed out for the bridge.

I couldn't tell right off if it was Em on the bridge. A truck made its way down the valley from the reserve side. A trail of dust followed the half ton for a brief moment before the morning breeze dispersed it.

The figure on the bridge stuck his thumb out but the truck sped past him on the bridge.

As I got closer I was starting to wonder if maybe I should turn back. The Em I knew would never want to catch a ride to town. She was totally self sufficient and would have no reason to go to town. That was over twenty years ago though, a lot might have changed by now.

I had to find out so I kept going. I could start to hear the river current it was a sound that beckoned like a welcome. I was nearly on the bridge and because of the current the stranger on the bridge still couldn't hear me coming.

The stranger was wearing a hoodie and was on his cell phone texting. I never owned a cell phone I was too old school and used a land line. I pretty much had to get in his face before he finally looked up.

It wasn't Em.

"How's it going," I stuck out my hand.

The kid looked like he was in his teens did this strange handshake using a combination of fingers, fists, and pounding his fist up and down.

I just wanted a standard handshake.

"Hey dude," the kid replied and was back on his phone.

I stood next to him looking over the rail. The river was quite low more sand bars exposed than before.

He fiddled with his phone for a while and then he put it away.

"Got any T3's?" he asked.

"What are T3's?" I replied. I knew what they were I was just trying to act like I didn't know.

"Never mind," the kid replied. He was fidgety just like the way I was feeling. I wasn't out of the woods yet my nerve was still not there.

We stood there quiet not knowing what to say or do.

I decided to break the silence.

"Are you from around here?"

"I just live up the hill," the kid replied.

"Where are you headed?" I asked.

"I'm waiting for my buddies they're coming this way from the reserve."

Soon as he said that a truck came down the valley road as if on cue. Once on the bridge the vehicle came to a gradual halt beside the kid. Before he got in the kid asked if I wanted a ride, I shook my head. He got in and the truck took off to the other side of the bridge.

Alone on the bridge I started to doubt my decision of coming home again. I had sustenance for a few more days so I decided to wait until then. I started the slow walk back to the house when I heard a voice from the bridge.

"Where did your cat go?"

It was Em a smile and few lines creased her face.

My old friend whom I thought I'd see again on much better terms was standing at the linear entrance of the bridge. We met and gave each other a hug.

"It's been a long time Em."

"Yes it has."

She stood back and examined me from head to toe. Her look of elation suddenly changed to a look of concern.

"I know. Believe me I left with the best intentions but as you can see I was left battle scarred. You still look the same a few lines here and there."

"I earned them," she replied.

We both looked westward leaning on the rail like we used to as kids.

"The reserve has gone to hell since you left. Gangs are running around and selling this new drug. Our people are dying from this drug that's supposed to be used on large animals. The ones that don't care anymore are taking this drug. Are own people are killing our own with this drug. This bridge is being used to transport this drug onto our reserve."

A car rumbled down the reserve side of the valley. The first of the afternoon bingo players was making their way to town. The car passed us on the bridge not even giving us a second look.

"She probably thinks we're junkies wanting a ride to town," Em said.

Minutes later another car came down the road.

"Let's go up to the house and have some tea. I'm not feeling too comfortable here on the bridge." I said.

"Okay."

"I've been working on an idea I want you to see what you think."

She nodded. She took out a cigarette and turned away from the breeze to light it.

I grinned.

"What?" she smiled.

"Some things don't change."

We left the assimination bridge. This would be the first time Em would come to the house. I guess she knew it had been empty for several years now. She never did give me a straight answer as to why she never visited me at my home. The same thing about her home in the trees she never invited me there either. When we were kids I repeatedly asked her about her family, she repeatedly said not to ask her. I gave up asking and just accepted it.

Things were different now. We were different people now. Everything was in crisis mode and Em and I had to get to know each other again. This time we were going to have to be open with each other. Em said many things before I left and I had to be straight with her about my time away.

We walked in silence following the faint trail in the tall grass I created when I first came back.

I waited for her question.

"So tell me about your time away?" Em said.

"Well as you can see from my withdrawal state I've seen better days. I fell into some traps I didn't expect."

"Did you finish school?"

"No I didn't. I found out you have to be a different person to make it out there. I thought I was different enough to make a difference. I guess I was wrong and it took this long for me to realize it."

"Well you came back and that's all that's important. I'm not going to say 'I told you so' I knew you'd come back when you were ready to come back. You don't have to explain anything to me."

More vehicles were making their way past us to town. Just like in true native fashion they all stared at me as they drove by.

"Oh yeah, how did you know about the cat?"

Em smiled and continued to puff on her cigarette.

"I'll tell you all about it, there's a lot I have to tell you."

"Me too, let's go in and do some catching up."

7

WE GOT INSIDE AND EM sat at the table while I prepared some tea. She looked around at the surroundings for the first time. There wasn't much to look at, the walls were bare and a calendar still hung on the wall. Em saw my notebook and began perusing the ideas I was jotting down.

"Those are the ideas I was telling you about. I think I figured out why I didn't make it in the city."

I sat down at the table while we waited for the water to boil.

"It's the bridge and everything that it stands for. Symbolically this bridge is our connection to the past and the future. The past is our holistic way of life on one side of the bridge. On the other side of the bridge is the linear future the white world. Today we have nowhere to go. We have a culture that is getting saturated from the linear side with each passing generation. We can't go back because the past is gone. Our pure culture separated from us when the whites landed on our shores. Since that time our culture has been steadily eroding."

"So how do we fix this problem?" Em said.

I paused and got up to take the water off the burner. I got the tea ready and poured us a couple of cups and gave her one.

"I identified the problem I just haven't figured out a solution," I replied and sipped on tea.

I had a question for her and it was about what the guy that gave me a lift had said. Em was real I gave her a hug. She was sitting at my table drinking tea and lighting another cigarette.

I didn't know how to ask her why the driver didn't see her all those years and only saw me. Maybe it was the driver himself that had a problem seeing Em. Maybe he was a recovering alcoholic most of the bingo players were former drunks. There were a lot of maybes that could explain what he said. When the time was right I would ask her.

"It's funny you brought up the bridge. There's a story about the spot where the bridge was built. I never told you this story before."

"Okay, you have my full attention."

"Before the whites landed on our shores there was a warrior who had heard through allies and enemies that the whites were coming. This warrior got word that the natives that came in contact with the whites got sick and died a slow and painful death. He was strong and fearless and had won many battles to preserve his people's way of life.

As the whites began moving closer natives from other tribes were being driven back toward the warrior's territory. Weak and helpless allies and enemies were literally dying at his feet. The warrior wasn't going to wait for them he was going to head toward them and drive them back.

Along the way the warrior came across another native sitting up against a tree. He rode up to the man and when he saw the man the warrior saw the last stages of the sickness. The man a strong virile warrior was shivering and sweating. The warrior could see the red dots all over the man's face. The man with his last bit of energy reached out to the warrior.

The warrior got off his horse and offered to hold the man's hand in his last moments. The warrior who had been strong all his life held the dying man's hand and wept. The warrior stared out at the prairie grass waving and rolling to the pulse of the wind.

He held the man's hand only long enough until the man drew his last breath. The warrior got up and wiped his eyes, inadvertently transferring the secret disease into his body.

The warrior rode on until sundown and stopped to rest for the night. He camped alongside the river this is when he started to feel weak and the shivers came. In the morning he barely had the energy to start again on his mission to fight the whites.

A couple of hours passed and the warmth of the sun could not break the shivering the warrior was feeling. He was now drained of all energy and was slumped over his horse barely hanging on.

It was at this point where the bridge is located that the warrior got as far as before he fell off his horse. The warrior knew his time was near. He wasn't afraid of dying, he was angry for the way the whites had defeated him.

With his last bit of energy he dragged himself to the river's edge and vowed he would get his revenge in the next life. The warrior went in the water and he never came up again. It is the very spot where the bridge is built."

"That is quite a story Em," I said and sipped on tea.

We drank tea in silence to let the story sink in.

"Why did you tell me that story Em?"

"I'm a descendent of the warrior."

"How does that make you feel Em?"

"Remember when we were kids I told you that I had special powers?"

"I remember, I kinda figured you had some kind of power.

I didn't then, but since I've been back I think you do. That's the only explanation."

"Explanation for what?"

"When I came out here I caught a ride with a guy and we had an interesting conversation. He said he remembered me from the bridge when we hung out there. He said he only saw me on the bridge all those years. He never saw you on the bridge and that didn't make sense."

Em laughed.

"Now I'm confused," She was laughing and I was in the dark about something.

"The people that crossed the bridge thought you were crazy because they always saw you talking to yourself. They couldn't see me that was one of my powers."

"Just like you knew about the cat."

"That's another power I have. I was the cat. You gave me water and some of your bologna. I kept those hungry spirits away so you could sleep."

I felt like I had just entered a new realm of reality. Knowing that this kind of power was possible felt like a release from the old world. I felt invigorated and enlightened knowing the possibilities of Em's power.

"If you had this power why didn't you do something about the problems on the reserve?"

"It's not that simple. You've been gone a long time, a lot has happened since the time you left."

"I'm sorry Em it's just that I'm hearing about this revelation for the first time. I'm jumping to conclusions you're right it's been a long time."

"Getting back to my story the warrior on the other side did not go away. He's gone from our world but he is still in the water in a different realm. His anger did not go away even after all this time. It's hard to explain but he created a world for himself in the water by using the power of his anger. The trick was he could sustain the realm as long as his anger remained strong. He died centuries ago and that's a long time to stay angry. When his anger power began to weaken the warrior found a way to attract others from the reserve into his realm when they died. Once in his realm the warrior helps them create a realm and fills them with his anger. Given the way the natives have been treated to this day it didn't take the warrior much to convince the natives his anger was legitimate.

To make matters worse every generation since his time have been dying younger because of the drugs and alcohol. The warrior waits for these natives once they have crossed over and intercepts their energy. Overdoses, car accidents, housefires, fights, sicknesses, these all are claiming our people and the warrior waits for them on the other side.

In exchange for the anger energy the warrior helps them create realms of their own no matter how beautiful, perfect, absurd, impossible, or perverted. The warrior is amassing power with this anger energy and plans on taking his revenge on the whites."

"How is he planning on doing this Em?"

"He's harnessing the energy of the natives that enter his realm. He's going to use this power to breach this world. With these natives being young they fall under his spell and he takes their life energy. The only ones that are immune to his power and persuasion are natives who lived a full and long life. It takes a full life to help you move on to the other side. A full long life gives you life lessons that help you and the warrior is powerless. The only problem is there are very few natives who reach old age so they are few and far between."

"You've known about this since you found out he was

your ancestor?"

"When they found out what the warrior was planning, our family have been watching and waiting for him. The power I learned has been passed down since that time. My uncle possessed the power and passed it down to me."

"So the warrior is right out there under the bridge. That is kind of freaky knowing someone like that is lurking. All this time we were hanging out on the bridge and the warrior was there probably waiting for us."

"You weren't in any danger," Em said.

"Were you looking out for me?"

"You were looking out for yourself by staying away from the drugs and alcohol and your determination to make it off the reserve," Em replied.

We finished our tea.

"It looks like we both have a situation on our hands Em."

"We both want to change things why don't we help each other?" Em suggested.

"I'll make some more tea and we can brainstorm some ideas," I said.

8

WE DRANK SOME MORE TEA and we just sat there and enjoyed each other's company. When we were kids Em and I would sometimes just stare at the river below. The sound of the current the rustling of the leaves had a calming effect.

Sitting here at my table I felt that same calming effect.

Em and I spent the evening and most of the night talking about old times.

I told her about the linear white world. In elementary school during recess it was the whites against the natives in a game of soccer. We put up a good fight, or should I say I put up a good fight, since I was the only native in the class.

Em learned that I felt the wrath of the school principal's rulers, paddles, and conveyor belts over my hands. I witnessed the teachers in junior high use baseball bats on students for being late. I told Em one teacher swung a student around by the hair in front of the class.

All the way through school the curriculum did not include anything about natives. Oh I forgot, there was some mention of natives in social studies class. I found out we were below the poverty line that was it.

There was no mention of the history of natives being trapped between the past and the future on the assimination bridge. I endured to the end of grade 12 because I wasn't satisfied with that. Only a handful of natives made it to grade 6 and either dropped out or returned to the native school on the reserve.

It didn't end there.

The university had programs designed to teach natives to be teachers. The curriculum was designed for natives to teach on the reserve. This was a popular program among the natives and it gave the native studies program a profile to keep it going.

The catch was if a student wanted to teach off the reserve the linear world wouldn't touch these teachers. The white school boards did not consider these teachers because they didn't go through the regular teaching program offered to white students.

I told Em about this one professor in an English class that purposely mispronounced my name. He would say, 'has everyone got, how about you,' and then he would say my name wrong.

It was late into the night when I finally got some sleep.

When I woke up Em was sitting at the table with the tea ready.

"So we have a common interest in the bridge," Em said.

"Yes, all we need to do is put our interests together. This power of yours enables you to be undetected by everyone else?"

"That's correct. My uncle and I lived in a cabin in the trees with the purpose to carry on this power. Our job is to watch over the warrior and make sure he doesn't breach this world with the power he's taking from the natives that cross over. I know hold this power once my uncle crossed over and it's up to me to watch the warrior."

"So I'm not crazy?"

"No you're not crazy, everyone else thinks you're crazy," Em replied.

"Great, I left hoping I could be an example. All this time people just thought I was nuts."

"So tell me some more about your ideas," Em said as she lit another cigarette.

"We're basicly trapped between the past and the future. Our present existence is on this bridge out there. The bridge is everything, our state of mind, the drugs and alcohol abuse, the violence, the unemployment I could go on. The only way we deal with this is we wait. We are powerless against the bridge so all we do is wait. Life on the assimination bridge is a form of waiting. We don't know we are waiting. We don't know what we are waiting for. We are the assimination bridge and we are assimilating parts of the past and future to forge an identity."

"So it looks like we both have a problem with this bridge,"

"If we can bring the attention of the assimination bridge to the reserve and to the whites maybe we can start some kind of discussion. At least shed some light on my idea. I came back with nothing and I so much wanted to come back to show you that I made it out there. Now I'm back and only a shell of what I used to be. All I have is this theory and I'd like to see if I can bring it to light."

"So how do you propose to do this?"

I sat back and drew a blank. Then it hit me.

"We need to bring the cameras and reporters to the bridge. Make it a publicity stunt, a press conference of sorts."

"Everyone thinks you're crazy that might work in your favor," Em added.

"Yes that's good we could use that. We're going to find a way to get the media and cops out here and we'll disclose the truth about the assimination bridge."

"Why the cops?" Em asked.

"The media follow the cops, where there's cops there's a story. Once we get to town we'll make an anonymous call to the media and reserve cops and say there is going to be a drug deal on the bridge tonight. As for the city cops we'll draw them out by getting them to follow me to the bridge."

"And how are you going to get them to follow you out here?"

"Everybody thinks I'm crazy right? I'll get them to follow me by stealing a car. I think I can make it out here before they can catch me."

"There's a good chance you'll get thrown in jail once you reach the bridge," Em said.

"I'm counting on the media and the cops on both sides of the bridge to show up all at the same time. Once we plead our case about the assimination bridge I'm hoping to get off lightly. There have been some clever people who have raised awareness through some clever means in the past. Some of the things I learned during my days at the university. There's so much history I learned about our people that's been swept under the rug. These are things that were never included in high school, and why would they when there were no natives in white high schools."

"What if this plan doesn't go as planned," Em said.

"My life didn't turn out the way I planned. I'm prepared to accept what happens. I have nowhere to go all I have is my theory. I want people to look at themselves and realize the waiting has to stop. We have to rebuild using what both ends of the bridge have to offer. The past is gone but use what is left from the reserve side of the bridge. We have to accept that the white side of the bridge is not going away. If we have to learn both sides of the assimination bridge to survive then that's what we have to do. I've identified the problem I now have to work on a solution. I believe there is a solution, if there wasn't a solution we'd be extinct by now. We are still here we didn't go away that means there is a solution. It might take some time but I believe things can be better for what's left of our people Em."

"I will help you with what you have to do. You didn't come back home empty handed. Maybe it took all that time for you to find your cause. Here on the reserve there is no such thing as a normal life like it is in the white world. All we do here is endure and react to our desperate situation. You went out there and came back and that's all that matters to me."

"With your help I think we can do this. All we need to do is catch a ride to town to get this plan in action."

"Shouldn't be hard today, it's family allowance day there will be plenty of traffic crossing the bridge," Em replied.

9

TODAY THE GRAVEL ROAD WOULD be busy with families going to town to buy food, to pay off pay day loans, to pay out items from the pawn shop, for dead beat dads to buy their drugs and alcohol.

It was also another day for the bingo and casino players.

Em and I started making our way to the bridge just before the afternoon bingo players were to make their way to town. Once there, it was a matter of catching a ride if anyone stopped for us.

We waited and within an hour several vehicles passed by without giving us a second look. Em and I were starting to wonder if anyone would stop and offer us a lift.

There was a lull and there were no more vehicles. Enough time passed the dust started to settle on the gravel road.

I think it was time to ask Em another question.

"Em I just realized I don't know what you've been up to all these years. Do you have kids are you happily married?"

She paused and lit a cigarette.

"This power was passed down to me and I had a choice to accept the responsibility or live a normal life. A normal life out here is not normal so I accepted the gift I was given. I was in a relationship about a year ago and it was getting serious. I took a ride with him to the reserve he was a child care worker. On the gravel road we got into a pretty bad accident. He didn't make it."

"I'm so sorry Em, I didn't mean for you to bring back any bad feelings," I said and put my arm around her shoulders.

"That's okay, it's been over a year. I've had some time to try to put things back together. He was trying to change things by working with kids."

"Did he know about your powers?"

"No, I didn't think he was ready for that. Can we talk about something else?"

"Of course Em, I didn't mean to…"

"It's okay. I'm just not ready to talk about him."

We stood there in silence again, feeling shitty about getting Em upset. In all the time that I knew her I never seen her get upset. I was always the one that got bent out of shape and she was always cool and composed.

More vehicles continued to pass us on the bridge. Then the silence came back when the vehicles disappeared up the hill. A lot had happened in Em's life and this was our first awkward silence we ever shared. When we were kids we could hang out on the bridge and be comfortable with each other and not say anything.

I decided to break the ice.

"So you're devoted your life to this power. That must've been quite a sacrifice," I said.

"Not really when you consider how things are on the reserve. My uncle transferred the power to me because he needed me to continue to watch the warrior. He's got these souls immersed in their fantasy realms while the warrior saps their life energy for himself. That's over a century of life energy he is harnessing for revenge. This descendent of mine is still angry after all this time. His anger is being kept alive by the life energy he is taking from our people. This publicity thing you're planning might be a way to draw him out of his realm."

"What do you mean Em?"

"I think with his anger getting the best of him he might attempt to come back and he might be vulnerable then. We could expose your theory to the media and at the same time we might be able to draw out the warrior."

"First things first we need a ride to town," I said.

As if on cue a black van came down the gravel road. The black van slowed down to a halt beside us.

"Remember they can't see me," Em said.

The sliding door opened.

Em got in first and I followed her. The door slid closed and we were off. The van had only two seats up front and the rest was cargo space. The first thing that hit my nostrils was the pungent smell of skunk dope. With the two up front and three natives in the back they passed around a joint. It came to me and I shook my head, it was then passed up to the two up front.

"They have rifles," Em whispered.

I took a quick glance and there were a couple of rifle butts sticking out from under a blanket.

"Where to?" the driver said as he glanced at me from the rear view mirror.

"I just need a ride to town," I replied.

Including the driver they were all probably in their late teens. Judging by the dope and rifles my guess was they were unemployed, unskilled, no ID, and were drop outs from school. They were content with the lifestyle they were leading on the reserve. They didn't know any better as a result they had no expectations or goals.

It was another example of the waiting on the assimination bridge mentality. These boys just like to get high and go deer hunting.

Worldly matters beyond the assimination bridge did not touch them and if they did it was beyond their comprehension. They knew they had no prospects on the reserve and they accepted this. They took generalizations and hearsay as fact just like most natives on the assimination bridge.

"Are you from around here?" the driver said.

"I left the reserve years ago I just came back," I replied.

"These boys are drug dealers," Em whispered.

"Ssh!" I whispered back.

The boys in the back looked at me their eyes slanted and grins creased their faces.

"They are playing out the realms that are waiting for them in the Warrior's realm. These boys don't have a chance and they are playing into the warrior's hands. She took a look at their stoned faces and started to laugh under her breath.

I looked at her and mouthed the words, "shut up!"

"They go into town on family allowance day, welfare check day, and old age pension day. These are the days when they go into town to get their drugs. Once they get their supply they go back to the reserve and sell their drugs," Em whispered.

I could hear her but I didn't want to acknowledge her in front of the boys getting high.

"You want to do us a favor?" the driver said.

I looked at him as he glanced through the rear view mirror.

"If I can, it's the least I can do for giving me a ride," I replied.

"We don't have any ID can you pick us up some beer when we get to town?"

"Yeah sure," I said.

"They don't carry ID in case they get stopped by the cops. They might even be on warrants for arrest so they don't carry ID,"

Em whispered.

It wasn't long before we got on the highway, from there it was only 10 minutes into town. I didn't want to be with them when they met up with their drug dealers. The less I knew about them the better it was for me.

I was hoping they would hit the liquor store first. Sure enough the first one here in the outskirts of town is where they pulled in.

The driver turned off the engine and handed me some cash.

"Get us a couple of cases of beer and a bottle of gin."

"You got it," I replied and got out of the van.

"We can make our phone calls here Em. We'll get their stuff for them and we can be rid of them."

"They are bad news," she added.

I went in and got their booze. I approached the van and the side door slid open. I handed the stuff to one of the boys.

"Thanks for the ride guys I'll be good here," I said.

"If you want a ride back we'll be passing through here in the evening," the driver said.

"Thanks again for the ride," I said.

"No problem," the driver replied. The sliding door slammed shut and the van took off.

"They are probably using family allowance money to buy their drugs. They sweet talk their young naïve girlfriends, or get them hooked on drugs so they can get their hands on the money. If they can't get the money then they steal it to get their drugs," Em said.

"Well it's a good thing we got off the van. We can't be getting involved with them when we have a plan to carry out."

I looked around at the surroundings and remembered this all used to be pasture land and farms. Now everything here is all subdivisions and strip malls.

"So much has changed around here. The school bus would pass

through here on the way to school and none of this was here."

"You lived in the city for the past twenty years you didn't see all the changes going on?"

"I went from my place to work and from my place to the bars and casinos. That's why I had to get out of there I was trapped. My goal of continuing school didn't work out and so I did the next best thing and that was joining the white work force. I thought it was work, get paid, and spend your money. I realized too late that it wasn't the case."

"Work is work what else can it be?" Em said.

"Here in the white linear world work is work on the surface. We're all doing the same thing working and spending time in the bar after work. At the same time they are paying mortgages, they are raising kids, paying property taxes, they are budgeting right down to the last penny. They don't have an assimination bridge to fall back on. They don't have a bridge where they can wait indefinitely. Even though I was working side by side with the whites I was still waiting and biding my time just like the ones on the assimination bridge. Even in the city I was trapped between the past and future. I brought the assimination bridge with me when I left. Look around Em all this doesn't belong to us. In the meantime we just wait."

"After tonight the waiting could come to an end," Em replied.

10

"WHAT DO YOU MEAN?"

"This plan of yours is going to put the cops and media at the same place. I'm hoping the warrior will show up once he sees the white cops. To the warrior the white cops represent the people that wipe out his own people. They are the ones he didn't get a chance to fight when their invisible weapon got to him first. I think with his anger still strong he might come out of his realm."

"How's that going to happen?" I urged.

"I don't know. I'm hoping the white cops will set him off and his guard will drop. I want to see if he can appear in this realm, with or without his realm still intact around him. If he somehow breaks free of his realm because of his anger then he won't be able to return to his realm. There is a lot of 'ifs' here but we won't know unless we try."

Em's plan was now dependent on my plan so now it was doubly important to carry it out. This whole thing was now in motion. At some point it was all theoretical but now with Em's input it was actually going to happen. There was still time to back out if I wanted to. This plan was important to Em for different reasons other than my own so we were going to go through with it.

Em and I caught a bus downtown to the seedier part of the city. Here in the outer suburbs we stuck out because it was all linear territory. Downtown in the older part of the city there was an area where natives congregated in a park area. In this area there were skid row bars that catered to street people, minorities, and natives.

The usual shops surrounded this part of downtown, pawnshops, tattoo parlors, payday loans, coffee shops, and confectionaries.

Em and I blended in well.

My co-workers and fellow university students would never frequent this part of the town. I never made it out here either but it was safe for Em and I. We needed to make some calls to get this plan in motion. A few blocks away out of the range of skid row was a mall. That was our destination so we headed that way.

The mall still had a row of pay phones and the steady flow of traffic made it easy to be anonymous. The first call was to the native police force on the reserve.

With the drug problem escalating on the reserve it was easy to get the attention of the reserve police. I informed them that I was anonymously reporting a drug deal going down at the bridge tonight.

The next call was to the city newspaper. In their bias nature they leapt at any headlines dealing with natives. If there was any wrongdoing dealing with natives they splashed their pictures and names on the front pages. I could almost hear them salivating over the phone when I told them a drug deal was going down at the bridge tonight.

The calls were made and Em and I left the mall.

"You only made a call to the reserve cops and the newspapers. What about the city cops?"

"I've got another plan to get them out at the bridge. Everyone thinks I'm crazy maybe we can use that angle," I replied.

"Some of the rumors I heard were you got sent to a mental institution all these years." She said.

"Well the life I led was slowly driving me off the deep end and I didn't even know it till it was too late. I might as well have been crazy to think that the linear world was for me. I was too proud to come home empty handed and chose a life that was a lie. I think I've finally put it into perspective with my "assimination bridge theory."

"So what is your plan?"

"We are going to steal a car Em."

"Why are we going to steal a car?"

"I'm crazy remember? It's the only way to get the cops to chase me to the bridge. Their jurisdiction runs right up to the bridge. This evening we'll catch a bus to the outskirts of town. We'll find a car or truck in one of the strip malls on the edge of town. From there it's only 20 minutes to the bridge. I will give them my name the white cops will confirm it with the reserve cops. Maybe the rumor will get out that I'm crazy this should make my plan more effective."

We made our calls and left the mall undetected. On our way out we passed a food court and even there I noticed that the natives were huddled in a small section of the food court. They were segregated and relegated to one small area. Was it by choice that they didn't want to be near the linear people? Were they huddled because they were harassed by the mall security? Either way the natives knew their place in the mall and that's how it was.

We made it back to the park area of skid row. There were plenty of park benches where we can hang out for the next couple of hours. When we got to the park Em and I can see the native drunks moving around in small groups. In this square block of park trees, green grass, and monuments the native nomads moved around like they were on display in a zoo.

Shoppers, business people, mothers and the linear population in general walked past the park and its nomadic people. No one ever gave the native transients and drunks a second look. The linear people knew better than to show any interest because this would be an invitation for natives to ask for money.

There was no avoiding the assimination bridge. The parks in the middle of downtown were an extension of the assiminaton bridge.

Em and I found an empty bench and we sat and watched the activity. A group would assemble and share a bottle passing it around before the cops knew what was happening. As the day passed the groups would divide up separating from the ones who were getting too wasted. The wasted ones would eventually pass out on the grass until the cops picked them up and hauled them to jail.

"All these natives look like they are in their eighties but they're only in their thirties and forties. The drink and substance abuse has aged them prematurely. The warrior is waiting for them. They won't get passed him because they are too weak. He will offer them a false sense of power and self determination and they will buy it. For once they will feel like they are in control, but its control they will give up." Em said.

Something caught Em's eye and she began looking behind me intently at a group of natives. She then quickly put her head down as if not to get noticed.

"Don't move!" she whispered.

I stood still facing her.

All the nomadic lost souls were oblivious and yet Em spotted something that was out of the ordinary.

"What is it Em?"

"I think he's here!"

"Who's here?"

"The warrior," she whispered.

Em moved her head to the side of me slowly to get another look. She started past me and hid behind a tree. I casually turned around and couldn't see a thing but the drunks in a group. There wasn't anything or anyone that looked out of place. From my peripheral I could see Em using trees and people as cover to get to the person she was after.

Standing there I could see the group Em was honed in on. There were three natives standing by a tree one was quite animated with his hands telling a story.

Em waited a few moments and then made her final attempt and started for the group. She quickened her pace and then she started running. I started walking towards the group but still couldn't see anything. The three continued in their conversation and weren't aware they were Em's target.

Em reached the area and saw me coming so she put up her hand gesturing me to stay put. I was still out of ear shot of the three natives so I couldn't hear them. The three continued in their story with Em standing there beside them unaware of her presence.

I slowly started moving toward her just close enough so I could hear her voice. She was definitely looking at someone or something that I couldn't see.

I stopped when I heard her start talking to someone that I couldn't see.

"I was able to come back because I survived. I was with Seth and you made the mistake of thinking I didn't make it." Em said replying to a question that was posed to her.

She waited as if listening to another question. She then replied again.

"It is physically impossible for you to come back. I think after all these years you don't know how to come back. All you can do is surround yourself with this energy you're stealing from your own people. Yes, I know what you're doing with the lost souls that come your way."

Em waited again to reply to another question.

She was listening and occasionally shook her head and sometimes nodded in approval. When she disagreed she would shake her index finger. She replied again.

"You have to stop what you're doing. If you say anger is energy and emotions are energy in your realm, they are energy here as well. You have to accept they work differently in your world. If it wasn't for the people you took, your energy of anger would have passed by now. It's no longer anger for you it has become something else. You want to live again and since you can't come back you are settling for the lives of your people to keep your fantasy going. I'm coming for Seth and I will find a way to free those energies you have stolen."

The conversation was over and Em started back toward me. She had some tears she was wiping away. This whole plan suddenly took a turn I wasn't expecting. Judging by her conversation I think Em was going to open up about the man that was once in her life.

11

"WHAT HAPPENED EM?"

"It was the warrior. He found a way to enter this world and still be protected in his realm. He can only observe our world because he's still protected by the realm from the other side. He can come here and check out the natives listen to their conversations and generally find out which ones are coming his way," Em explained.

"I didn't see anything,"

"What gave him away was his shadow," Em replied.

"His shadow?"

"Yes, your shadow is dark. In his world his shadow is a source of light because our day is their night. Our day is their night and his shadow was casting an orange glow. I caught him by surprise and instead of retreating to his realm he waited to see what I had to say. He knows who I am and he said he was ashamed to be related to me. He said anger is like a source of power in his realm. I think his anger and his thirst for revenge is driving him crazy even after all these years. He slipped up when I ended up in his Seth's realm because he thought I was killed in the accident too."

"What accident?"

"His name was Seth the man I was in a relationship with. Let's go we'll talk someplace else."

"I'm getting hungry let's head for the soup kitchen it's only a few blocks away."

"From the looks of it the warrior's been visiting this place where native drunks hang out. By listening to their conversations he can get an idea of what they are like. He can find out their stories, their weaknesses, and their hopes." Em said.

When we got to the soup kitchen we were just in time for some lunch. Em and I got served some food and we found a table. We tried our best to sit isolated from the others but it wasn't going to happen. Most of the transients wore hoodie type sweaters and toted around bags.

We drew some stares because we never visited the soup kitchen before. One in particular kept looking our way and sure enough he picked up his tray and came to our table. His tray was empty and wanted to check us out before he left.

"Are you guys heading out to the reserve?" he said.

Em shook her head and kept eating her sandwich.

"Got any change for the bus?"

She shook her head again.

I took a few bites and realized something. This drunk native was talking to Em.

"He was talking to you Em," I whispered.

"You don't have to whisper. I can still appear to others if I want. I was hungry too, besides how's it going to look if all anyone saw was a tray of food floating beside you. I guess for some of these drunks that go through DT's that would be normal."

"You're right Em that's good thinking. I've heard some of these drunks can see some crazy things when they go through DT's."

"You can stop whispering they can see me," Em said.

"I forgot. Force of habit."

No one else bothered us as we had our meal. Only a few white transients were in the soup kitchen. The rest were from the reserve all across the demographic the young and old. They were all trying to escape the assimination bridge. They didn't know what they were running from all they knew was the waiting, waited for them at the assimination bridge.

So they were here in the city moving around like nomadic people trying to find the next high. Drugs, alcohol, hairspray, rubbing alcohol, it didn't matter as long as they were numb to keep the waiting at bay.

We finished our meal and left the soup kitchen trying not to draw any more attention.

"The plan is set Em all we have to do now is kill a couple of hours. If we walk to the outskirts of town that should take a couple of hours, but I don't feel like walking. What do you suggest Em?"

"Let's hit one of these coffee shops and sit or awhile. We'll pick a booth and I can tell you about Seth. I've haven't talked about him since the accident. It's only fair I give you the whole picture because in a way he's part of my plan."

Skid row had plenty of coffee shops we kept walking until we saw the first one. It was sandwiched between other small shops that lined this particular street.

We entered.

It was relatively empty with only a few patrons having coffee. I picked a booth away from earshot so I could engage in a conversation with Em.

The lady brought coffee and went back to her counter. She was occupied with a reality show on a small tv.

I sipped on my coffee and leaned back to relax the tension in my neck and shoulders. The tension was always there in recent days, it never occurred to me to just simply relax my shoulders until now.

It was quiet between us neither of us wanting to say anything. We both looked out the window and sipped on our coffee.

Em finally broke the silence.

"Was there a lady in your life?"

If Em was going to talk about her friend then it was only fair that I tell her about my time away from the reserve.

"I was serious once. I met a girl at the university she was white. As it turned out our common interest was drinking at the local bar. We went out when we first met and then we went out again the night before she left. In between that time we took some of the same courses and spent lots of time in the bar. When she decided she was going to move away she wanted me to go with her. I couldn't just drop my studies so she left and I stayed. Since then I've met a few girl's mostly just acquaintances at work and at the casino. Nothing serious since my days at the university, the best ones are usually taken. That's the price you pay for being single I guess."

"Seth and I met on the bridge. I was on the bridge and I started noticing him cross the bridge. I asked around and I heard that he was a child care worker on the reserve. I decided to come out of my shell and appear on the bridge for him. He stopped and asked if I was okay. We struck up a conversation on the bridge. From there we got to know each other. He believed in equality in all things. This was the quality that I liked about him. He believed that there was no reason for two people to fight if they deeply cared about each other. He said the opposite qualities of two people made them almost as one. Seth said our wants and needs should complement each other for a good relationship to exist. He was the one I thought. When I lost him I thought he would be strong enough to not get trapped in the warrior's realm. It was his belief in equality that the warrior used to trap him. I know I can't get him back all I can do is to free him from his illusion."

"How can equality be used against you, isn't equality a good thing?" I said.

"Equality in a perfect world is a good thing but you and I both know that it not true in real life. The warrior created a realm for Seth where everything is equal. For that his energy was taken by the warrior. I suppose a realm where everything is equal is not a bad thing compared to some of the realms the others are in."

"You have visited these realms Em?"

"With my power I can see the realms but I'm on the outside looking in, just as the warrior can see our world and not intervene. If you left this world as an addict, alcoholic, gang member, or dead beat dad what kind of realm do you think you would want. It would be a pretty warped world and believe me when I tell you; there are some crazy insane realms under the warrior's control."

"I wonder if there is a way to enter these realms and convince these souls they are trapped and must be freed," I suggested.

"There is a way to breach their world," Em said and she lit a cigarette.

"You're not supposed to light a cigarette in here," I whispered.

"It's okay I'm lighting it to explain something," she held it up and let the wisp of smoke take flight whipping like a cat's tail. Em then put it out before anyone detected the smoke.

"What's your point Em?"

"Smoke is the power I can use to breach the realms. When I ended up in Seth's realm it was instantaneous. We were blindsided by a drunk driver we didn't see it coming. One second we were in this world and the next second we were on the other side where the warrior was waiting. Smoke holds a power and it allowed me to return. As a result my living body recovered. I believe if I stayed in Seth's realm my physical state would have died. It was then that I realized what the warrior was doing with our people and their life energy. I need to free Seth from the prison he can't see. There's just one problem."

"What's that," I replied.

"I don't know if entering the realms would affect my physical body in any way. My soul my energy would be leaving my body and I don't know if that means I would be physically dead. This has never been done to my knowledge. My uncle transferred this power to prevent the warrior from breaching our world, not the other way around."

Em noticed a couple staring at us so she stopped the conversation. I turned and looked and they turned away. It was time to leave the coffee shop. The time was getting close and the sun was starting to set. I paid the tab and we left before we drew any more attention.

Once we were outside it felt like we had no place to go. I never stole anything in my life and here I was trying to figure a way to steal a car.

12

"IT'S TIME TO HEAD BACK to the outskirts of town. We'll get on the bus and transfer to the edge of town. That should take some time and get us closer to our plan Em."

"I agree it's time," she replied.

We headed for the bus stop. Along the way Em went incognito again but kept puffing on her cigarette. She would quickly hand me her cigarette when someone passed us on the street.

The passersby would glance at me and I could sense their disgust. I felt like telling them I went to school and was a taxpayer just like them.

Em and I got on the bus.

We killed some of the time and before we knew it we were back at the original place we started at this afternoon.

It was a strip mall the one where we got dropped off this morning. Em and I stuck out because we were in a white neighborhood. We just leaned back on the building checking out the vehicles for a potential ride to the reserve. White folks would pull up do their business and were off again. No one stuck around long enough to be a potential stolen ride.

Em puffed on a cigarette. I looked at her.

"Are you visible or should I be looking for a hand off just in case," I whispered.

"I'm visible," she replied.

I realized I never stole a car before. I didn't know how to break into one. I didn't know how to start one without the keys. It looked so simple watching it get done in the movies.

It was getting close to the deadline without much time to waste. There was only one way this was going to happen.

"We're not going to steal a car Em, we're going to hitch a ride and then borrow the car".

"Who's going to give us a ride in this neighborhood," she said.

"That's a good question we'll just have to see what kind of situation presents itself," I said.

Em and I waited while vehicles came and went. The dollar store was getting the most customers so we decided to case the vehicles stopping there.

The vehicles continued to come and go.

"What are we waiting for," Em asked.

"We need someone with a truck, a cell phone, and a very cooperative driver. Who are the most trusting and vulnerable people Em?"

"The elderly," she replied.

After casing a couple of potential elderly drivers they ended up being the least trust worthy. They also didn't carry cell phones.

By some luck we didn't have to approach someone for his services. A kid probably on some errand to pick up a few things pulled up and entered the dollar store. He gave us a quick glance and entered the dollar store.

Em and I didn't give his quick glance any weight. It was one of those glances given to make a mental note that we were out here. If we were up to no good he could make an identification.

When the young white kid came out he got in his truck without giving us a look. I expected him to back up and be off on his way. He pulled up beside us.

"You need a lift buddy?" he asked.

"As a matter of fact I do," I replied.

"Where are you headed?"

"Just to the outskirts of town I'm headed to the reserve," I replied.

"I can get you as far as the outskirts get in," the boy said.

I looked at Em and she shook her head giving the signal that she was not visible to the white boy. Em jumped in the truck box and I got in front.

"We don't get many Indians in this part of the neighborhood."

"I remember this whole area being pasture land when I was a kid," I replied.

"Actually I'm not from here I'm down here visiting relatives. I'm from Ireland."

"You must be from out of town nobody calls us indians around here anymore. We are natives, first nations, aboriginal, or for the super ignorant, drunken natives. Before we go do you have a cell phone?"

"Who doesn't," the kid replied.

"You're right what was I thinking. Thanks for the lift,"

We were off and I could see Em in the back gesturing for a cigarette. I shook my head but she kept insisting bringing her two fingers to her lips.

"So what is this reserve you're going to?"

"It was supposed to be a temporary laboratory for us, it ended up being our homeland for the past 200 years."

"Why don't I just take you there, past the outskirts you'd have no light. You could get hit by a car."

"I wouldn't be the first native to get hit by a car on the highway trying to get home," I said.

"Let me give you a lift home to the reserve I'd like to see what a reserve looks like."

"It doesn't look like much in the dark. I got an idea do you smoke?"

"Yeah," the kid pulled out a pack of smokes from his coat pocket.

"Can you pull over?"

"Yeah sure," the kid replied and pulled over to the shoulder.

By this time we near the outskirts with only a few street lights ahead of us. The rest of the highway was darkness ocassionally lit up by passing traffic.

"Can I have one of your smokes?"

The kid lit a cigarette and handed it to me. Em was standing outside my window waiting for her cigarette. This was going to take some explaining.

"What's your name boy?"

"My name is Rory," the kid replied, totally unaware that his world, his reasoning were going to be challenged.

"Rory, regardless of what I'm about to show you, we will still need that ride to the reserve. We are going to need your truck with, or without your help."

I rolled the window down and handed the cigarette to Em. Rory followed the cigarette as it left my hand and seemed to float on its own outside the window. The lit end began to glow as if someone on the other side was puffing on the other end. Rory could see no one taking a puff. Smoke blew out of the night like someone exhaled.

In his state of shock I knew I had the kid in my grip.

"Rory this is Em and I'm going to get out and let her in to the truck. Are you still with me?"

The kid nodded still fixated on the lit cigarette which had a life of its own. Em got in with the cigarette still in her mouth and sat between us.

"Rory can I see your cell phone?" the kid took his phone out and handed it to me. I waited for him to get a grip.

"You look like you could use a smoke," I suggested.

The kid took out a smoke his hands trembled a bit. He was able to relax enough to light his cigarette. He took a puff and that seemed to calm him down a bit.

"Maybe he'd feel better if he saw a person on the other side of my cigarette," Em suggested.

"I don't know Em. Let's give him a little more time."

Rory took his eyes off the cigarette and looked at me.

"Rory would you feel better if you saw a person on the other side of that cigarette?" I said.

13

THE KID WAS STILL TRYING to get a grip of watching the floating cigarette glow from Em's inhale and puff. His reality just like mine when I learned the truth of Em's real existence came crashing down. In my case I was exhilarated by the possibilities of Em's powers. For the boy this was stuff made in the movies, and he was still trying to connect what he believed was real and what was happening in front of him.

"One step at a time Em I don't think he's ready for you," I suggested. "Let's not lose sight of the plan," I added.

"Okay," I turned to the boy, "Rory I'm calling the cops. I'm going to say that I stole your truck and I kidnapped you doing it. You have a choice you can get off when they get within sight of us. Or you can come for the ride and drive back to town once we get to the reserve. The decision is yours."

I wasn't sure if it sank in because the kid was still staring at the cigarette.

"The cigarette is still bothering you I can see. I think it's time for you to show yourself maybe it will help."

"Okay, divert his attention for a few seconds," Em instructed.

"Rory check your side mirror is that the cops coming?"

The kid glanced at his side mirror taking his attention away from the lit cigarette. When he turned back to me he jumped at the sight of a native woman sitting between us. Instinctively he jumped out of his truck at the sight of the woman that wasn't there a moment ago. I got out and went around to make sure he didn't wander onto the highway.

"Rory!" I shook him to make sure he was still breathing.

"I'm making the call are you in or out. We're still only in the outskirts maybe you should just walk back to town. The walk will help you get some fresh air and just forget about what you saw. The cops will bring your truck back I promise we won't put a scratch on it. What do you say?"

The boy blinked and looked at me showing some life for the first time.

"I will drive you and…"

"Her name is Em."

I made the call with Rory's cell and it was out. It was a matter of just waiting for them to appear on the horizon.

"No turning back here," Em said.

"It's going to happen Em," I replied.

"What's going to happen?" Rory asked, his ability to talk was coming back. He was coming back to his senses. I still didn't know if he accepted what was going on with the cigarette or the strange woman suddenly appearing in his truck. It didn't matter for now because the plan was now in motion. We had the truck and all we had to do was get to the bridge. The boy didn't factor in the situation we didn't have time to figure out if he was okay or not.

"Can you drive kid. Maybe I should drive since I know where

we're going."

"Maybe you're right," the boy replied and went around the truck to get inside the passenger side.

"Last chance Rory you can still get out of this. You don't have to worry about your truck you'll get it back."

"No, I think I'll join you and your friend. I can see that something special is happening here. Whatever you guys are up to I want in," Rory replied.

"With cops it can get dangerous just letting you know. Also, Em's got something planned for the bridge which she refuses to talk about."

"It can't be as crazy as watching a lit cigarette floating around in the air, or a woman, suddenly appearing out of nowhere," Rory said while he waited for the cops.

"With Em and what she's capable of, don't bet on it," I replied.

We could hear the sirens but still not within our sights. I told Rory to start going. It was a few more kilometers on the highway before we would make a right onto the gravel road. That road took us to the reserve about another ten kilometers.

I told Rory to pick up his speed to give us a safe cushion so the cops wouldn't overtake us before we got to the bridge. In the night we could see the flashing lights appear it was two cop cars.

By the time they got to our original spot we were at the gravel road turn off. We took the right and blazed up a trail of dust once we hit the gravel."

"When we start heading down into the river valley we should see flashing lights on the other side of the bridge," I said.

"And if we don't?" Em replied.

"Then our plan is shot."

"Not quite, my plan will be the backup," Em replied.

"You still don't want to tell me your plan Em?"

"It depends on the warrior and if he will take the bait. I don't want to say anything in front of the white boy he's still not sure about what's going down right now."

Behind us in the cloud of dust the sirens wailed and the flashing lights appeared translucent. I can see the lights shooting out into the fields on both sides of the gravel road.

We were really starting to move I was hoping no deer would get caught in our head lights. We made that last turn before the descent into the river valley.

"Slow down the road is pretty rough going down. The road going down goes right, left, and right again."

We still had quite a lead on the cops but they were gaining quickly on us. Going down the twisting turning descent we temporarily lost sight of the cops.

We reached the bottom and when we cleared the last turn Em pointed at the reserve cops already blocking the reserve side of the bridge.

"Just remember Rory you are our hostage we made you drive us out here. There's no reason for you to get into any trouble."

"I got it," his reply was marked by the thick accent he tried to hide earlier. Rory was zoned in on the situation at hand keeping his cool as best as he could.

We cleared the final turn and half a kilometer away was the bridge.

Rory began slowing down the white cops were now making the descent behind us. The Irish boy pulled up to the entrance of the bridge blocking the road way.

"Leave your head lights on and stay in your truck," I instructed.

Rory nodded staring straight ahead at the flashing lights on the other side. Em and I got off and slowly made our way to the center of the bridge. Once there a spot light lit up and illuminated us.

The city cops arrived and a few more were making their way down into the river valley.

"It has finally happened Em."

14

EM AND I WALKED TO the center of the bridge. Spot lights and flashing lights decorated the bridge sending a kaleidoscope of colors into the valley night. There were media people with cameras on both sides of the bridge right on cue.

The reserve cops on one end and the white cops arrived on the end, both sides trying to sum up the situation. No guns were drawn they had a look of puzzlement, maybe wondering if they had been duped.

No one on either side of the bridge seemed to want to take charge. No one had any idea of who had jurisdiction over the bridge. Jurisdiction was something I never considered. The bridge was forsaken just like the existence of the assimination bridge.

A cop on the reserve side broke the silence and said something to the cop next to him.

"I know who he is?"

"Who is he?" replied the other cop.

"He's that crazy kid that used to spend all day on the bridge talking to himself. I thought he was locked up all these years."

"Maybe he escaped from the mental institution."

I was getting insulted by rumours. I looked at Em and she was grinning.

"I'd give anything if you could show up in front of all these cops so they can shut the hell up about that once and for all."

Em nodded, "I agree. Well it looks it's your move," she said.

The parties were all here so I waved at them.

"I'm glad you came and you are correct I'm the kid that all that time on the bridge. I'm not crazy and I didn't get sent away. I went to school at the university and I joined the work force in the city. All these years I was paying taxes so you cops can get a pay check. That's not why we're here."

Upstream alongside the river's edge there was a spot where we used to go swimming during the summer holidays. Now it became a spot where people would light a bonfire and party.

The boys that gave Em and I a ride this morning pulled in there to roll some joints and have a few beers. The boys were taking it easy when all of a sudden their escape was cutoff by the reserve cops. It was okay for them because the reserve cops usually left them alone.

What started freaking them out was when they saw the white cops coming down the white county side.

The boys had all these drugs and some of them had warrants out for their arrests on previous charges. They were freaking out seeing all these cops like some sort of raid was going down.

They kept quiet and continued to monitor what was unfolding on the bridge.

It was time to state my case.

"I spent twelve years in the white catholic school system. I tried the post secondary system which was supposed to be my dream. I tried to show that there was a chance out there beyond both sides of the bridge. It turns out I only had half the credentials. This bridge this construct I'm standing on, that I spent most of my childhood, is the dividing line between my two identities. On one side I belong to a fading culture that I can't reclaim. It started to disappear the moment first contact was made. My other identity was out there in white land. I tried their dreams, their rules, all I discovered was I didn't fit there either. I ended up going nowhere fast living the fast of excess. Drugs, booze, and gambling all that took over because it helped pass the time when I wasn't working. I'm here to declare my new existence my new identity. I am a member of a new culture called the assimination bridge. Nothing below but the passage of time as the river current takes it away. Our aim to uphold this new identity is to wait. I wait for the fading forces on one side and the assimilating forces on the other side to decide my fate. I am part of both but belong to neither. I am half holistic and half linear and both sides are unrelenting. I am my own culture my own person, my own religion, my own government, my own law. Whatever happens to me tonight on this bridge won't change me, because both sides of this bridge created me."

The boys in the van listened intently as my voice reverberated over the flow of the river. One of them without the others knowing, picked up one of the rifles in the back of the van.

The boy brought it up and began scoping the scene through the sight of the rifle. The others were oblivious as they sipped on their beer and continued to listen in on the proceedings.

"It would be so easy to take out one of those pig cops," the boy whispered to himself.

"I think it's time," Em said.

"Time for what?" I replied.

"I put a bullet into each one of those rifles,' she said.

"What rifles?"

"The ones we saw in the van this morning," she replied.

"Why are you telling me this now?"

"Because one of those boys has just crossed the line."

Out there in the dark by the river side the boy squeezed the trigger wishing what he thought could happen.

The crackling sound he pretended would happen became a reality like thunder slamming down in the valley when a storm hit.

The boys wheeled around dropping their beer and joints. One of them grabbed the rifle out of the stunned boys hands.

The bullet ripped through the night and hit the steel railing next to the white police.

A silence fell on the bridge and doubt and vulnerability suddenly filled the tense air. Youth, naivete, and inexperience on both sides of the bridge could not hold the moment.

Not even two hundred years of quiet tolerance and ignorance could suppress that innate conflict that so began when the whites landed on these shores.

One side felt betrayed by the other and it didn't matter they were protectors and upholders of the law.

"They're shooting at us," someone in a uniform screamed.

It was always there that hatred between the two opposing sides on opposite ends of the bridge.

I'm not sure who fired first it didn't matter, all that mattered was that Em and I were in the direct line of fire.

When the flurry of bullets started cutting through the night air the yelling and screaming added to the chaos.

I felt a burn on my shoulder that sent me spinning. Another piercing burn sliced my side. Em grabbed me and we both went over the railing.

An ancient distrust was unleashed and cops started exchanging gunfire from both sides of the bridge.

Years and years of pent up anger awakened another force that swore to avenge his people. The warrior could not help himself watching his descendent Em and I being mercilessly cut down without a chance of fighting back.The warrior never got a chance to fight back he was cut down before he even knew it.

Tonight the warrior was going to get his chance at getting back at the white warriors.Thousands of wasted life energies over the years the warrior had harnessed for this one chance.

Life energies from the assimination bridge cut short, unfulfilled and unrealized, were now at the warrior's disposal.

In the night air over the river the warrior broke the threshold and raised a gigantic wall of water. It was intention to destroy the white cops, the white army he never got a chance to fight.

With one stroke the warrior raised the water and flung it toward the white side of the bridge. I could see this wave of water in its fury moving toward the white cops and then it stopped, as if in suspended animation.

The warrior's anger got the best of him and it was the chance Em was waiting for. Expending all that energy breaking through the threshold and raising the wall of water taxed the warrior's power.

All the while I was being carried away by the current. I could see Em on the bridge her arms raised. She was using her powers holding the gigantic tidal wave at bay buying time for the cops to escape its path.

The warrior's power began to weaken so he retreated back into the threshold from which he came.When the cops on both sides of the bridge were safe from the line of fire Em let gravity take over and the water collapsed.

The displaced water caught up to me and I swept further away from the bridge. All I could hear was the yelling and screaming.The din gradually faded as the swell pushed me further down the river.

I couldn't swim and yet I was floating numb with the pain from the wounds I sustained. I was always afraid of looking up into the night, and there I was looking straight into the unknown.

I don't know how long I was paralyzed by the pain and fear. I finally lost consciousness calling out in vain for Em.

15

I OPENED MY EYES THE pain was gone and it wasn't cold anymore. I was in some kind of cabin and a wood stove in the center was keeping me warm. I don't know how long I was out it must've been awhile because I was hungry. When I tried to move I was reminded of the wounds I sustained on my side and arm.

Slowly I got myself in a sitting position so I can have a better look at my surroundings. The woodstove was crackling and the smell of sage permeated the one room cabin.

Someone was coming to the door. I was too incapacitated to try and get up in case it was the cops. All I could do was wait and see who was coming to the door.

Em came in with some firewood.

"You're up," she said and put the firewood by the stove.

"I didn't know where I was I was starting to worry."

"I grew up here I took it over from my Uncle."

"Is this the place you went home to when we were kids?"

"Yes it is. We are way out nowhere in the trees along the river. No one knows we're here," Em reassured me.

"What do we do now Em?"

"It's been a few days the cops are not looking for you. They think you got shot and drowned. They managed to explain the wall of water that came down on the bridge. Some scientific bullshit that every one bought. Your speech worked it's got everyone on both sides of the bridge talking about the reserve. With your presumed death the message hit even harder. I guess you can say you're a martyr."

"I don't know if I'd go that far. My assimination bridge is just a theory. It doesn't matter anymore I'm officially off the grid."

"Does this mean you're giving up?"

"I don't know what else I can do Em. I'm dead to the world. I feel in some weird way relieved. It's like I've been given a second chance."

"What do you remember about that night at the bridge?"

"I remember saying my piece and then all hell broke loose with those trigger happy cops," I replied.

"Do you remember me telling you about the boys in the van?"

"Yes now I remember, were they the ones that started it all?"

"Well actually I started it all I put the bullet in the rifle."

"You sure know how to break the ice Em."

"Do you remember seeing the wall of water on the other side of the bridge?"

"Yes what caused that?"

"You didn't see the warrior?"

"No," I replied.

"He came out of his realm because he couldn't hold back his anger and he raised the wall of water to crush the white cops. I was able to hold off his attack and stopped the water. All this activity caused the warrior to lose some of his power. He's now weak and he needs new life energy to gain back his power. I'm going to go after him while he's weak."

"I'm going with you Em."

"Your place is here you can't enter the warrior's realm," she replied.

"There's nothing for me here I've been written off as crazy and dead."

"You need a plan Em maybe I can help you out. We could brainstorm this together. Maybe there's way we can get him to enter my realm?"

"But you don't have a realm you're still with the living."

"He wants to come back maybe we can get him here out of his element," I said.

"You might have something," Em replied.

I was hungry so Em prepared some food and tea. Together we began to brainstorm about stopping the warrior while we had the chance. After the meal Em sat opposite of me across from the wood stove and proposed an idea.

"The warrior is weak and he can no longer sustain the realms he has in his grip. I want to go in and free as many of the lost souls he has. They need to continue their path to the seventh star. I need to free Seth from his illusion so he can continue his journey."

"What about you how are you going to come back?"

"I don't know. All I know is I need to free the life energies in the warrior's realm while I can. He has to be stopped now."

"And what if you can't stop him Em?"

"I'm just like you. You're trapped between two worlds so am I. I've been to the warrior's realm and I belong in this world. The only way he wins is if I permanently leave this world. I don't intend on leaving this world without passing on my knowledge to the next one."

"Someone to take your place?"

"That's right. So far I haven't found someone. The person will come to me. It's usually someone that is still young like I was when

I was given this gift. That's why I intend on coming back here. I'm going to need your help with this."

"What do you want me to do Em"

"I need you to look after this place, make sure no one finds out about it. You can stay here and work on your theory because you have people talking about it. I will bring writing material for you to use. I will go out and bring you food and keep you informed about what's going on out there. For now you have to rest and let your wounds heal."

I was still pretty weak and once I had some food I decided to lie back down. The crackling fire and the rustling leaves in the wind outside seemed to lull me back into impending sleep.

I was in that stage where I was almost out and yet still aware of my surroundings when I heard Em say she was leaving. I acknowledged it and then I was out.

In the middle of the night I came to. The fire was still going and I noticed across the stove Em was sitting on the floor. When I sat up and looked at her she was in some sort of meditative state. I just observed and didn't want to disturb her. She must've have noticed I was watching her so she came out of her trance.

"Em?"

"You're up," she responded.

"Yeah I'm just a little thirsty," I said.

"I'll get you some water," she got up and poured me some.

I gulped some water down, "I thought I heard you say you were leaving."

"I paid the warrior a visit," she said.

"Wow, how did that go?"

"Many of the earlier realms he captured have faded and the life energies have released themselves. They are now on their proper journey to the seventh star."

"You mentioned that before the seventh star, what did you mean by that Em?"

"Look around you and you see transition in nature. Trees shed their leaves and new ones appear every year. Our life to the next is merely a transition to the next stage. The warrior could no longer hold on to these life energies and their obstacle was removed. Their energy resumed their next journey to a star out there. Stars are energy, we came from the stars, our physical make up came from out there. Our bodies are made up of the same things that are out there. Our life energy goes through a life stage here and our life energy moves on when the physical body runs its course. Right now the warrior is existing in the recent realms because they are still fresh in the life energies that have just entered his realm. The warrior has only a limited place to hide so I'm going after him and release my Seth from his grip. The recent realms are still strong and these energies are going to be hard to reach to convince them that their new existence is wrong."

When she said she was leaving I didn't actually see her leave. Em said she was leaving again and I waited for her to get up and use the door.

"I'll be back later in the morning to check your bandages and prepare some food," she said.

I waited for her to leave. She didn't leave she sat back down and closed her eyes. When Em left she took a route that I was not expecting. Given what I had seen she was capable of, I should have expected her exit to be extraordinary.

Em got into her meditative state and before my eyes she vanished behind wisps of smoke. She mentioned smoke before and its power.

16

WHEN THE SMOKE DISSIPATED EM'S energy was gone to pursue the mad warrior. She had established a bridge of her own between her world and the warrior's realm. For a brief time she was with her Seth and they crossed together. Everyone was fooled the warrior, Seth, and even Em. For that brief time Em became part of Seth's realm where the warrior was waiting.

Em could sense everything in this new realm was wrong. She survived the accident and that was the sense that was telling her she needed to leave. She came home to her body and the bridge between the two worlds was established.

The warrior was weak and it was time for Em to go after him. As long as she was alive she would be able to return from the Warrior's world.

Her body remained in a meditative state across from the woodstove.

She had a realm to destroy and I had a realm to save. Lives in both realms were at stake. I don't know what Em's plan was this was her realm to deal with.

I had mine.

The assimination bridge was going to become the assimination realm. There was a realm here in this world to test my theory on. I had a lot of work to do to pull the assimination bridge into the assimination realm.

The first step was to accept that we were existing on the assimination bridge. From there we could move onto the assimination realm.

So much to put on paper.

www.ingramcontent.com/pod-product-compliance
Ingram Content Group UK Ltd.
Pitfield, Milton Keynes, MK11 3LW, UK
UKHW040031200726
13854UKWH00001B/464